Bowly Can Celebrate his Mistakes

OH YEAH!

A Growth Mindset Story
by Angharad Davies

The Positive
Motherhood Project

First published in 2025 by The Positive Motherhood Project Ltd

www.bowlycan.com

© 2025 Angharad Davies

ISBN: 978-1-7390947-3-7

For the amazing children who helped create this book. Your plot ideas and emotion words were hugely creative and immensely fun. I had a blast.

Thank you!

Hello there!

I can't seem to find my friend.
His name's Bowly McLight.
He's a little light-filled bowl.
We were supposed to meet up here.

Hold on.
What's this ball doing here?
I wonder...

Here you are Bowly.
It looks like you kicked your ball over the other side of
that large ravine and now you can't get it back.
It also looks like you've tried getting across by making
a bridge out of pencils, but it didn't work.
I can see you're feeling frustrated.

Is that a stone I can see in there, blocking all your light?
A stone normally comes when you're feeling frustrated,
doesn't it? I bet you want to get that stone out and let your
light shine again.

Harrumph.

Golly! What are you doing, Bowly?

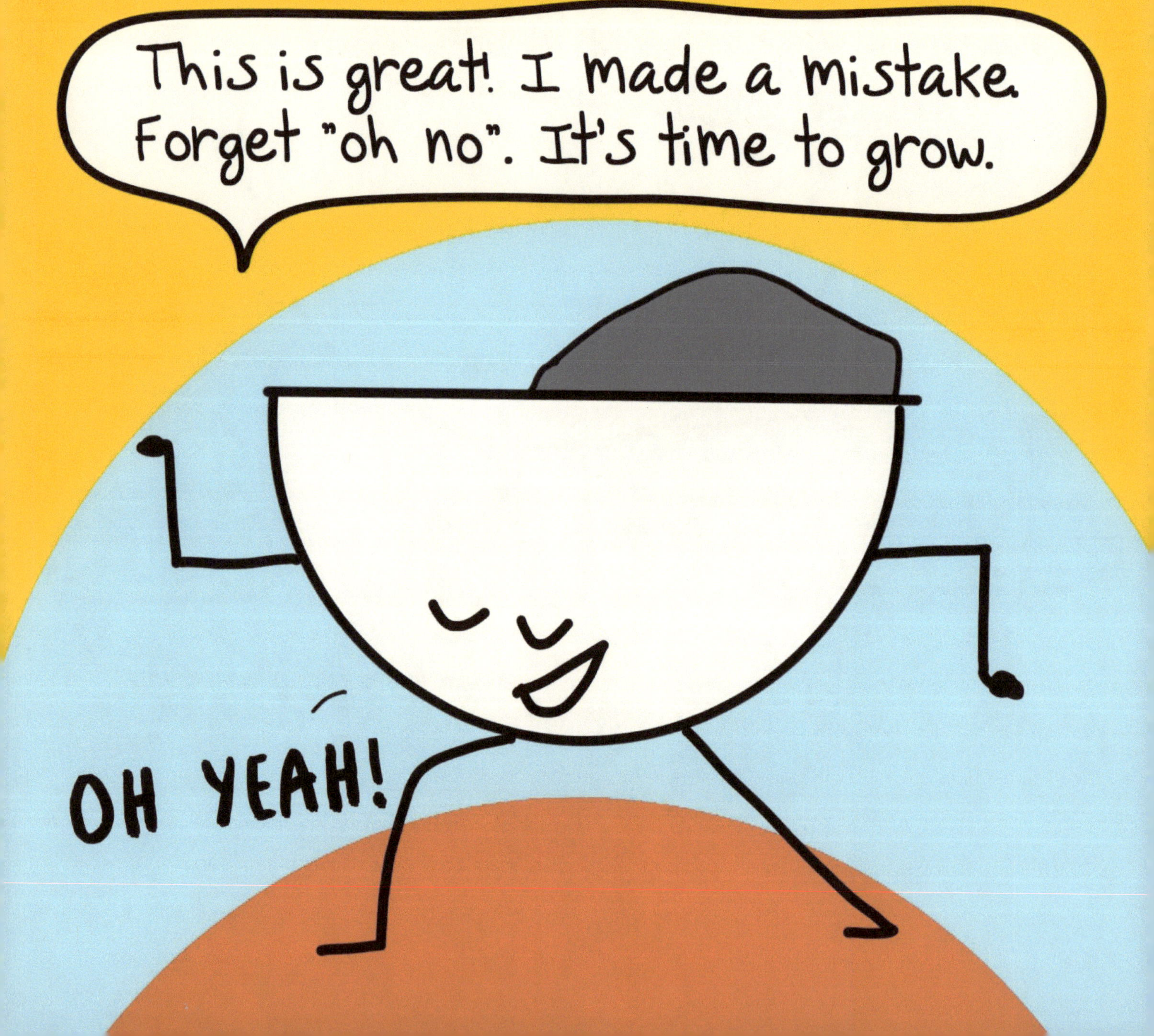

Oh, I see. You're celebrating your mistake.
And now you're looking inside your bag.
I wonder what you're looking for.

O-ho!
Toilet roll.

Ah, yes. Toilet roll certainly is longer
than the pencil bridge, Bowly.
You learned from your mistake.
Your stone flew out and your light
is shining again!

Blimey, Bowly! It didn't work.
I can see you look disappointed.
You have a stone blocking your light again.
A stone sometimes comes when you're
feeling disappointed, doesn't it?

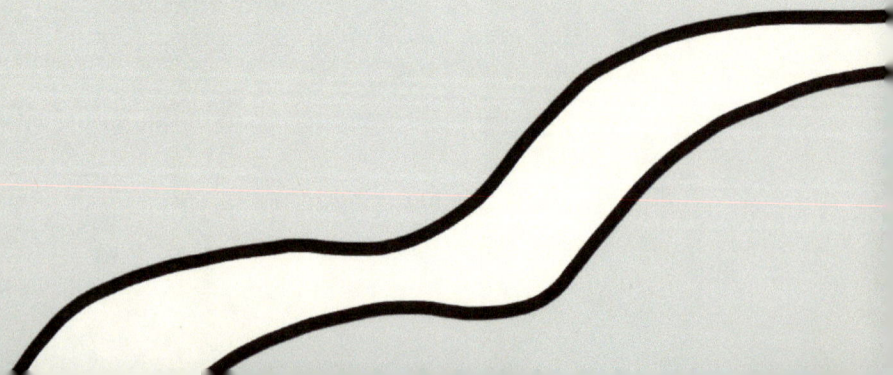

Phooey.

What's this? You're celebrating again!

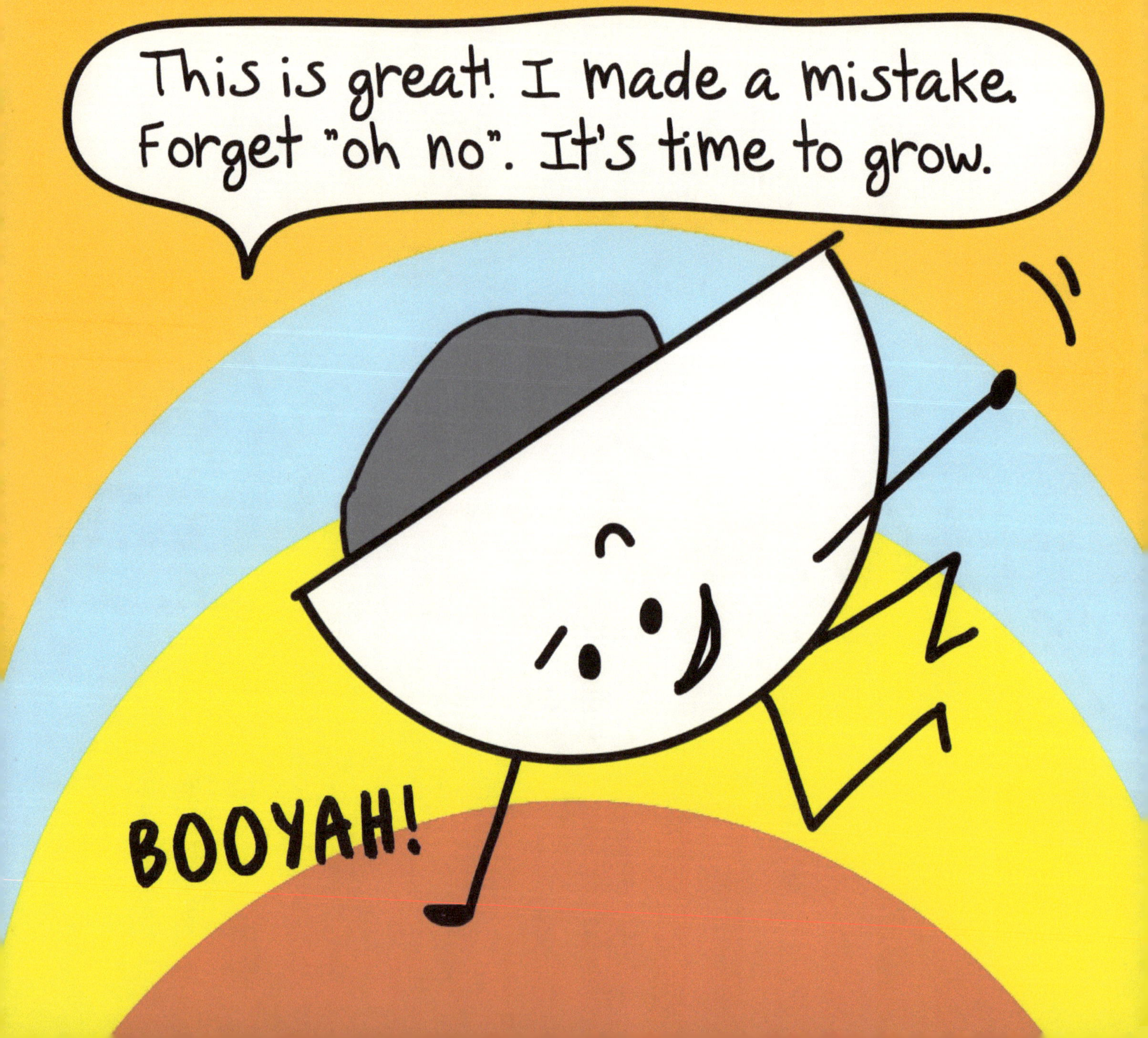

A-ha!

Mega mega chocolate bar.

Crikey, that certainly is stronger than the toilet roll and longer than the pencil bridge. You've learned from your mistakes. Your stone has catapulted out and your light is shining again!

Wow, it worked!
You made it across the ravine
and you can play ball again, Bowly.
Looks like you're busy having fun.
I'll let you play a while and come
back to see you later.

Three sunshiny hours later...

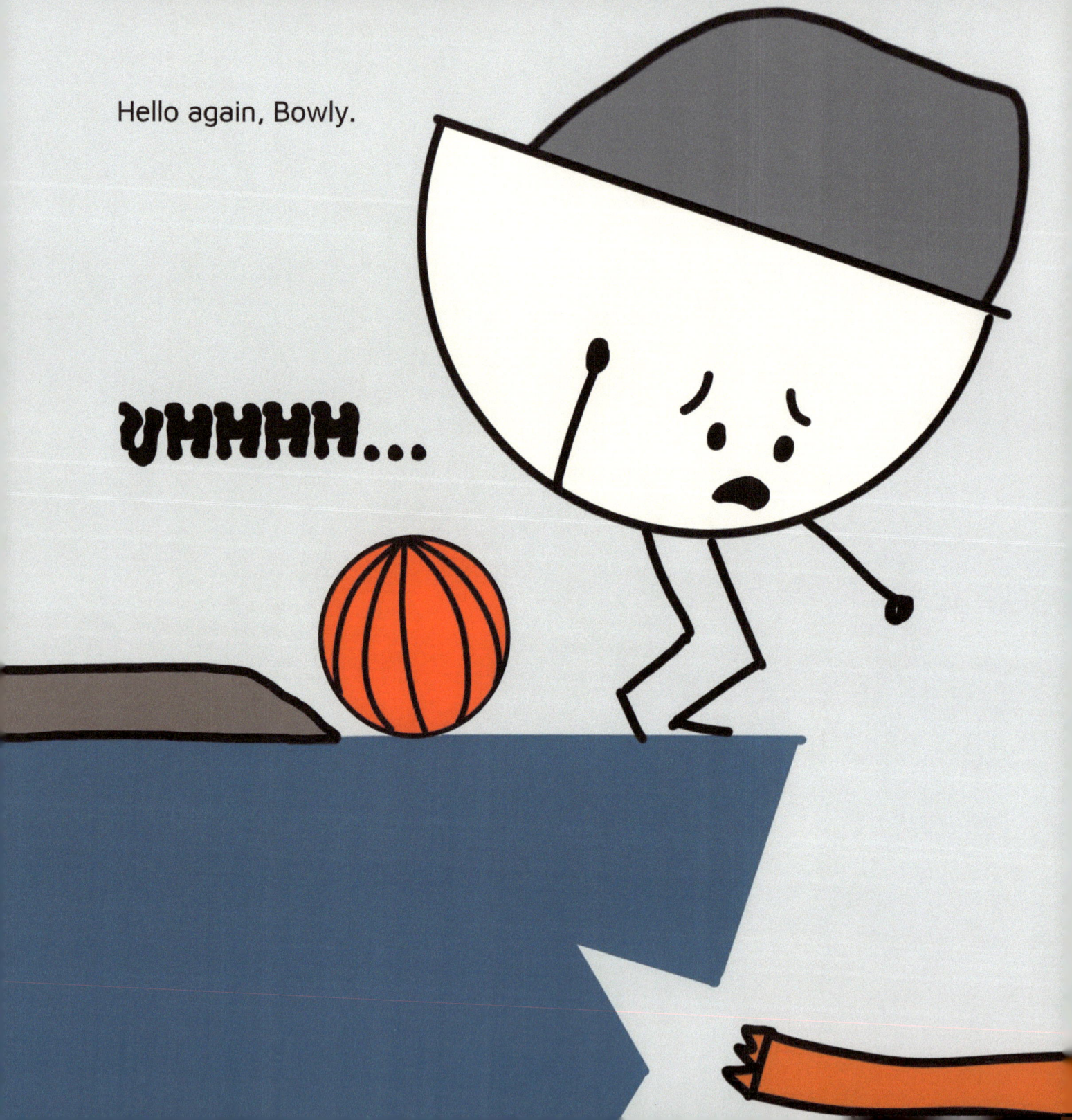

Jumping jellybeans! What's this?
The chocolate bar has melted in the hot sun.
Now you're stuck on this side
of the ravine and your bag is on the other.
You look worried and you've got a
humongous stone blocking your light!

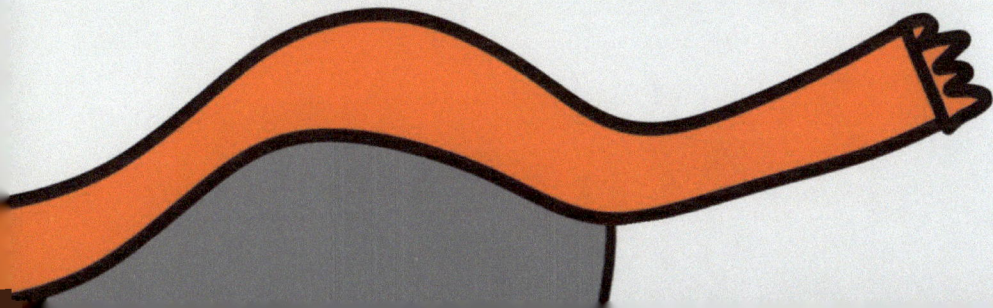

It looks like you've spotted something that
you can use to get back across, Bowly.

Great! A log. Come on then, Bowly.
It'll be dark soon. We should be getting home.
What are you waiting for?

Hmmm...
look before I leap.

Oh, I see. You learned from your last mistake
to think a little more before doing something.

AYYIIIIIEEEEEE!

Great big chomperooni!
Good job you looked because I'm pretty sure
that is NOT a log. Quick! Do something, Bowly.

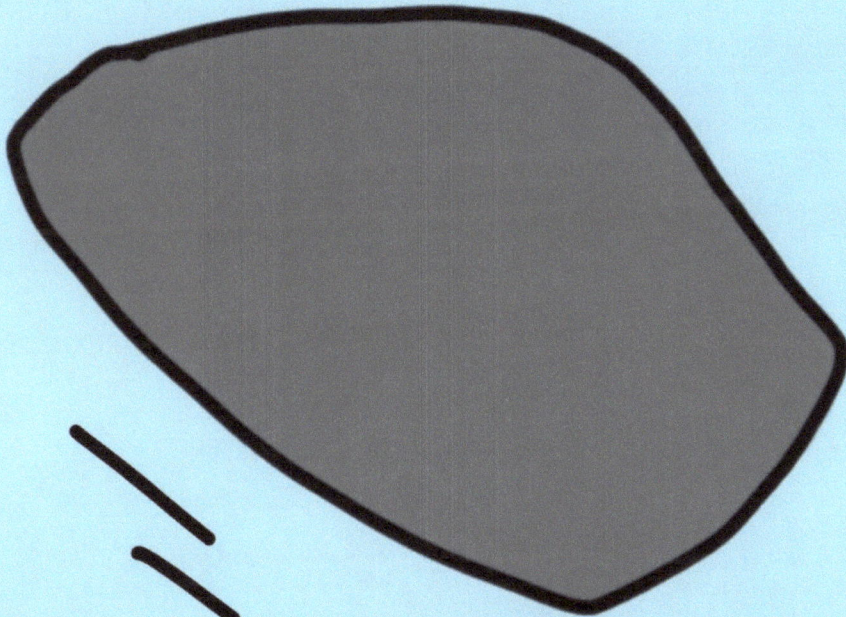

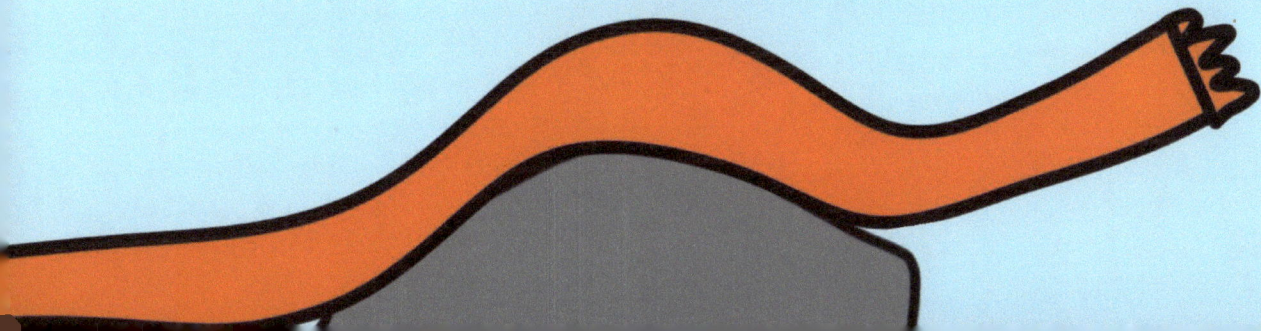

Wowee, Bowly!
You used the stones of your past mistakes
to get yourself out of that big pickle.
Look, your light is shining again.
I think it's time we continued this celebration
back at home, safe and sound. Let's go.

Huzzah!

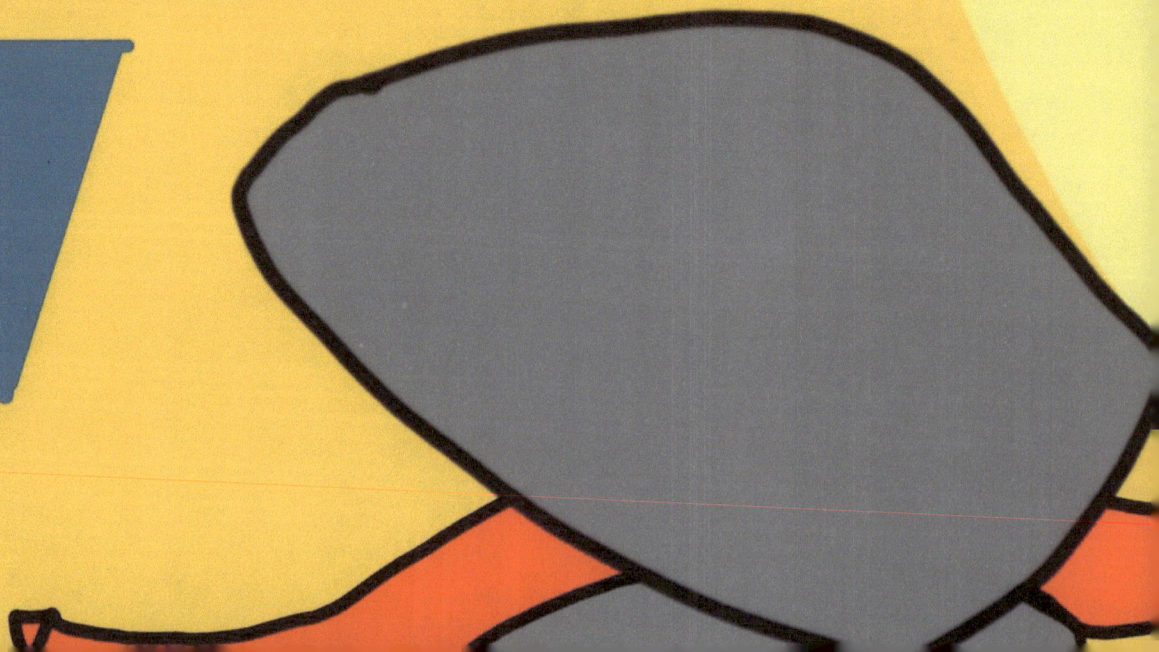

They say two heads are better than one. So what about hundreds of heads??

This book was inspired by the amazing plot ideas and emotion-conveying words brainstormed by children across the UK. Check out the schools and families that took part here:

www.bowlycan.com/mistakes

If your family, class, school or organisation would like to be part of the next book-creating project, please sign up here:

www.bowlycan.com/f/project

About the author

Angharad Davies lives in the UK with her husband and two sons. After witnessing the magic of story in her own children for nurturing emotional intelligence and resilience, she decided to write her own.

Combining her knowledge from postgraduate qualifications in Psychology and Play Therapy with her children's love for humorous reads, Bowly McLight was born.

Witnessing her children's enthusiasm and involvement in her first three books, Angharad knew more children needed to experience the behind-the-scenes of book creation. She is thrilled to now be making her books alongside families and schools across the UK – sharing this magic with hundreds of children.

About Bowly

Bowly was inspired by the Hawaiian teaching of the Bowl of Light.

He is fun-loving and adores a challenge. He wears his big emotions on his sleeve and is on a mission to teach children everywhere the coolest of tools, so that they too can face anything life throws at them - even big dragons!

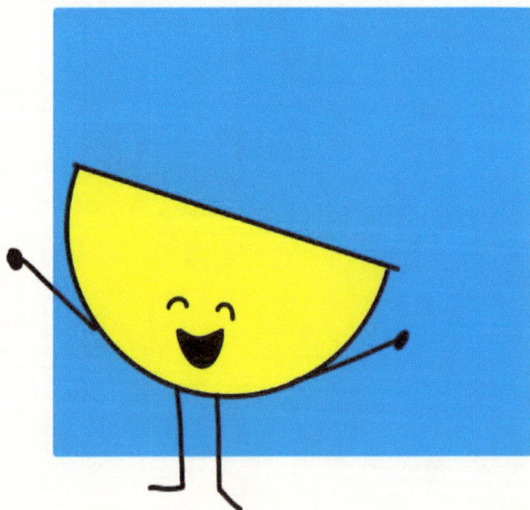

A new tool in every story

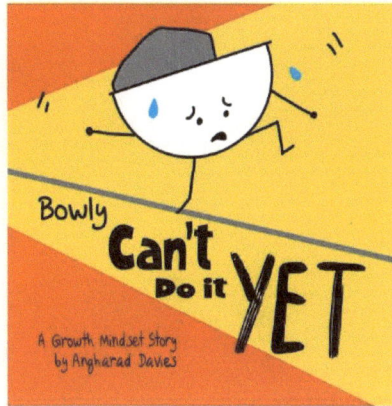

Bowly is feeling frustrated and is ready to give up learning to walk the tightrope when a mysterious word appears. Where did it come from and can it help Bowly to keep going?

A charming story to introduce children to the power of *yet* and learning to persevere when things get tough. The perfect book for helping children to build resilience and growth mindset.

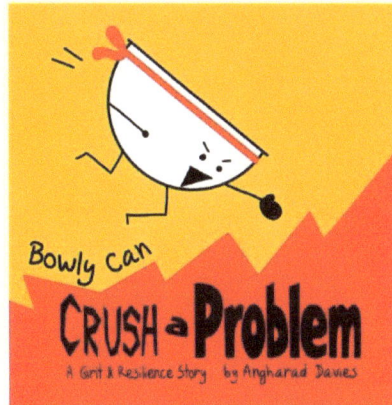

Bowly faces challenge after challenge, but never gives up. He has a karate-chopping-problem-solving trick up his sleeve! There's nothing that can stop him, except a dragon maybe.

A super fun story to teach children a powerful question when faced with a problem: *"What's the hard part?"* The perfect book to help nurture resilience and a solution-focused mindset.

www.ingramcontent.com/pod-product-compliance
Lightning Source LLC
LaVergne TN
LVHW072108070426
835509LV00002B/74